A Testimony to the G
in the life o

JAMES NAYLER
1618-1660

by
Dorothy Nimmo

Sessions Book Trust
York, England

© Dorothy Nimmo 1998

First published in 1993

Second impression in 1998

ISBN 1 85072 129 7

Cover design from a tile picture by Maggie Berkowitz.

Printed in Plantin Typeface
by William Sessions Limited
The Ebor Press, York, England

THE LAMBS WARRE

AGAINST

The Man of SINNE.

The end of it, the manner of it, and what he wars against.

His { WEAPONS, COLOURS, KINGDOM.

And how all may know whether they be in it or no; and whether the same Christ be in them that is, was, and is to come, and their faithfulnesse or unfaithfulnesse to him.

LONDON,
Printed for *Thomas Simmons* at the *Bull* and *Mouth* near *Aldersgate*, 1658.

Acknowledgments

SOME SECTIONS OF THIS poem have already appeared in *Stand* and *The Rialto*.

I am grateful for the help of the libraries at Haverford College and Pendle Hill, Pennsylvania, Friends House Library and the Bodleian Library, Oxford for help with research and to the Joseph Rowntree Charitable Trust for making this edition possible.

ONE

Walk cheerfully over the world
answering that of God.

What question do you imagine is being asked?
What do you think would be acceptable as an answer?
Who do you think is asking the question?
Do you think the answer will be the same
yesterday today and tomorrow?

Read the question carefully before you attempt to answer.
Answer cheerfully.

You might have found footnotes helpful.
Indeed you might have found footnotes
more interesting than the body of the text
which flows down the page
like a river thick with silt
difficult to navigate
treacherous with snags, sandbanks, gulleys
and sinking sands out in the bay.

The question is of James Nayler
called the Quakers Jesus
who suffered at Old Exchange.

A Warrior in the Lamb's War.

TWO

Most people know about the fear
but most are afraid. They look
the other way, think about
other things because after all
they have to live.

But the Warrior stays with the fear
until he is all fear,
until the whole of his mind
heart soul strength
is in the fear
and then he will change
then he will go through
and come to the clarity.

Some people know about the clarity
but most are afraid. The light
gets in their eyes, they dazzle,
they would rather not see so much
because after all
they have to live.

But the Warrior stays with the clarity
until he is fully clear
and the whole of his mind
heart soul strength
the whole of his life
is in the light.
Then he will change
then he will go through
and come to the courage.

Not many know about the courage.
It is not something they need to know.
They watch a few set out
not knowing where they are going
and think they are going too far.
Most would rather not.
They have to live.

> But the Warrior stays with the courage
> until the courage is all of his mind
> heart soul strength
> the whole of his life
> which he will give up
> and go through
> and come to the Cross.

THREE. Wakefield, 1651

JAMES NAYLER. Born in Ardsley
two miles north of Wakefield, 1618 perhaps
but the records are lost. Of his father
nothing is known but that he was a farmer
(sow-gelder, some said, but that was slander).
Of his mother nothing is known.

> (As for his education it was such
> as would make him capable
> of any ordinary employment.
> He was a man of exceedingly quick wit
> could write a very legible hand
> and spell good English.)

At twenty he married Anne of whom
nothing is known.

They had three daughters in three years.
Then James joined the army; Cromwell's army,
the Army of the Saints. Independents, Levellers,
Ranters, Baptists, Anabaptists, Brownists
Fifth Monarchy Men. It was this army
who cut off the King's head in Whitehall
on a public scaffold.

So the world turned upside down.

Over nine years James was promoted Quartermaster
under Colonel Lambert:

(He was a very useful person. We parted with him
with great regret. A man of unblamable life
and conversation, a member of a very sweet Society
of the Independent Church at Woodfield.)

but was discharged for reasons of health.

FOUR

GEORGE FOX: born in Fenny Drayton, 1624.
His father Righteous Christer, weaver,
his mother Mary Lago
of the stock of the martyrs.

George (a child of unusual gravity
and stayedness of mind) had trouble reading
(perhaps already resisting the letter
preferring the Spirit?) so instead of the Church
(which might have seemed suitable
for he knew purity and righteousness
and the Lord taught him
to be faithful in all things)
they sent him to a shoemaker and dealer
with whom he prospered. At nineteen he left home
and (having gone through all the professors)
Jesus Christ spoke to his condition
and he came up behind the flaming sword
into the Paradise of God, the innocency
Adam himself was in before he fell.

Never looked back. Never. Never.
Pure as a bell. Strong as a tree.
When George says Verily
none can alter him.

FIVE. Lichfield, 1651

GEORGE FOX.
I was one time walking
when I lifted up my head
and espied three steeple-house spires.
They struck at my life.
I asked what they were,
they told me Lichfield.

    He was moved to take off his shoes
    to have a sense of all conditions.
    Small stones under his heels
    a prickling of rough grass
    a spark of thistles
    and the cold striking up from the ploughland.

    He was not a man to spare himself
    and did not spare others.

    Three spires dancing against a white sky
    over wet fallow fields bare in October.
    George walks barefoot across country
    into the town where the blood is running
    out by the gate. The square's awash with blood
    the lambs are bought and sold,
    the lambs are bleeding
    the lambs have no defence and Fox
    paddles through blood crying WOE!
    WOE TO THE BLOODY CITY OF
    LICHFIELD!

    The fire of the Lord burns in his feet. He washes
    blood from between his toes, from off his shins
    reclaims his shoes and strides
    roughshod and does not feel
    small stones, grass, thistles. So passes
    through the country about Wakefield.

SIX. Wakefield, 1651

Flat country. Heavy land. Time
to break ground and James is at the plough
meditating upon the things of God. Hears
God's voice. Clear as a bell. He's glad,
had waited all his life long to hear it.
Obedient hands the farm over to Anne.
Is ready. Waiting. Waits.

He is not well, can't eat, sleeps badly,
hides his head under the coverlet at night
to shut out his imaginations. In the shed
hens are squawking, down the meadow
lambs call and are answered. There are
scratchings at the gate, rustling in the haymow.
A hen's feather floating on a bucket.
A cockerel crows. Fox is about the place.

>What is thee waiting for, James?
>Hast lost thy leading?

>When it is more pain to stay than to go,
>when you are like to die if you stay as you are,
>when you have no choice,
>when it is time
>you will find yourself going.

So when the time comes James goes gateward
saying farewell to none
going Northward to the savage parts
not knowing today what he will do tomorrow.

>Watch Fox racing away over the stubble
>bearing the fire in his tail.
>Cut swathes flare out in the early twilight
>smoke hangs as a sign over the roadway
>morning the fields are scarred with black windrows
>and small creatures are smoked from their burrows.

>Fox, running before the pack, knowing the coverts
>gets clear away and heads up Pendle.

SEVEN. Wakefield, 1651

ANNE NAYLER.
James off Northward Monday, left plough out
and field half done. Set Tom to finish,
did well but slowly. Headlands rough.
Trace broke where it was cobbled,
will have to be replaced.

Good year for apples. Set pigs to windfalls
and dung the orchard. Calves looking grand.
Wethers to market, prices only middling.
Ten pounds of apple cheese. Cleaned ditches.
Rain. Sarah still poorly.

EIGHT. Pendle Hill, 1652

FOX
up Pendle Hill
dark fell
witchcraft and filthiness
he climbs (with much ado)
fast as a fox and from the summit sees
over Ingleborough
beyond Sedbergh

LIGHT
strikes bleached limestone, bedrock, bones
of land laid bare under long rains
dry bones raised up and
far off
seaward
westerly sunlight on wet sands
streaks bright under black sky.

LIGHT
though nightfall darkness
covers sheep lost in hard times
all winter long hurdled within black walls
under the frozen drifts the lambs
picked out by great black crows
and the shepherd an hireling

FOX
sounds the everlasting day
gathering the Seekers to the fold up Firbank
into the LIGHT
aflame
ablaze
and in the blessed LIGHT
SO STAND.

NINE. Swarthmoor, 1652

Howgill says, The Kingdom of Heaven did catch us
as in a net. Margaret Fell says
We have taken the Scriptures in words
and know nothing of them in ourselves.
John Camm says, You could have knocked me down
with a little apple. George Fox says
Christ saith this and the Apostles say that
but what canst thou say?

James says nothing.
Richard Farnsworth says nothing.
But they were both there that summer
though when the story is told and re-told
(Margaret the Mother in Israel,
George her dear father in the Lord,
Swarthmoor the Birthplace of Quakerism)
James and Richard are indistinct
dark blotches in the shadow of a rock.

At Walney Island, in the foreground, George
(who has enraged the crowd) is dragged from the boat
beaten and stoned, forced to retreat to sea.
They have to send a horse to bring him home,
he can scarce turn in bed he has been so used.

James, in the distance, scrambles up the fell
half hidden in bracken but the crowd
stream after him. Do they catch up with him?
Is he much hurt? How does he sleep that night?

Dear George, writes James,
from Kendal, Mallerstang, Stainmore, Barnard Castle,
Dear Brother, cease not to pray for me.
I am brought much to silence within myself
and a willingness there is to be nothing.

Dear George. A willingness there is
to be nothing.

TEN. Appleby, January 1653. Examination upon the
charge of Blasphemy.

Put off your hat.
You are in contempt of Authority.
Authority commands you to put off your hat.
What do you say to that?

> When God commands one thing
> and Authority another
> I obey God.
>
> Concerning the Scriptures,
> none can rightly understand the Scriptures
> but they that read them in the same spirit
> that gave them forth.
>
> Concerning the Lord's supper,
> if you intend to sup with the Lord
> let all your eating and drinking
> be in remembrance of him.
>
> Concerning the resurrection,
> those who cannot witness the first resurrection
> within themselves
> can know nothing of the second
> except by hearsay.
>
> Concerning the Baptism; the baptism I own
> is of the spirit. Those that have been baptised
> into Christ
> have put on Christ.

Is Christ in you?
Is Christ in you as a man?
Do you own the Christ that died in Jerusalem?
Did Christ ascend into heaven or no?
Was Christ a man or no?
Was Christ the Son of God?
Are you the Son of God?

> Christ is a mystery and thou knowest him not.

SENTENCED: to be committed to Appleby prison
for the space of three months.

> I was made to refuse their diet
> and since then have lived upon bread and water.
> I see myself as a sign
> to a people wholly given over to the lusts of the flesh.
> For this is my liberty
> whereby the Lord sets me free above all created things
> and no freedom until then.

ELEVEN. Wakefield, 1653

ANNE NAYLER.
Appleby for James. Two days there and back
over by Stainmore. High poor country.
Black-faced sheep. A bitter wind.
James off his food, says the Lord keeps him.
Two trees down round back when I got home.
I set Tom to them, firing for winter.
Finished the ham. All the girls poorly.

TWELVE. Appleby, 1653

His voice sounds out of the low prison
(he hath a very commendable gift of oratory
and a delightful melody in his utterance)
over the hills in the teeth of the wind
drifting snow in the lee of the walls
where the lambs find shelter.

THE LAMB'S WAR (writes James
in a very legible hand and spells goods English)
THE END OF IT THE MANNER OF IT
AND WHAT HE WARS AGAINST.
THE WAY ALL FLESH COMES TO KNOW THE LORD.
A WORD TO THE SEED OF THE SERPENT.

Released in April he goes
where the Lord wills.
Sedbergh, Mallerstang, Kendal,
Rustendale, Swaledale, Shap,
Barnard Castle, Pickering, York,
Staithes, Holderness, Balby,
Brighouse, Pontefract, Lincoln,
Derby, Chesterfield, Nottingham.

And lifts up his voice:
A DISCOVERY OF THE WISDOM THAT IS FROM ABOVE.
A WORD FROM THE LORD.
SALUTATION TO THE SEED OF GOD.
A DISCOVERY OF THE BEAST
FOOT YET IN THE SNARE.

And again and again
in dear love
he writes to George.

Dear Brother how dear thou art to me
words cannot now declare.
Dear Heart cease not to pray for me
the work is great and many temptations.
As thou art moved let me hear from thee
that I may be kept in the Lord humble.

Dear Brother I have received thy letter
I rejoice. Oh dear friend, be faithful.
Let me hear from thee as often as thou canst.
Let me know where thou art
that I may come to thee.

Forget me not, my beloved one.

THIRTEEN. Wakefield, 1653

SARAH, HANNAH, MARY.

Our Father which art
not
there.

Our Father which art absent
which art absent-minded
not all there.

In a world of his own
always.
Not of this world.

We are all of us
children of God. Our Father
is about his Father's business

but our Mother is about
the house and about
the yard.

FOURTEEN. London, 1655

Now is the Lord raising up a People in London.

The expectation of Friends is very great
to have some Friends out of the North.
The burden is great,
we are too few for this service.

Let none come to London
but in the clear movings of the Spirit
Let none come to London
but those that are raised up in the Spirit of Truth
for there are so many mighty in London
so many rude apprentices and Ranters
that none but the Power of the Lord will chain them.

>Someone will have to go to London.
>James, you are IT.

James is very serviceable here;
many great ones flock to see him.
He is fitted for this great place
and a great love is begotten towards him.

FIFTEEN. London, July 1655

We hear you James Nayler
we are not sure we understand you.
Your accent is strange, being from Northern parts
and your matter extreme though not entirely unfamiliar.
You will have read Boehme and perhaps
Benet of Canfield? We know George Fox
has a copy of Niclaes' Speculum Justiciae.
Do you know Dr Pordage? Winstanley? Nicols?
This is a direction in which many are moving,
Collier, Saltmarsh, Wilkinson, Bauthumley.
We are eager to hear you but feel it wise
not to support you publicly. We remain
hidden behind the panelling.
Where do you stand upon Perfectibility?
Are you aware of the Doctrine of Castellion?
Of the Grundletonians, like you from Yorkshire?

> Dear Lambs, you cannot understand the Word
> except you go through and beyond the words
> and into the Silence.

Do you own the Christ that taught in Jerusalem?
In the flesh?

> The body of Christ I own is real flesh and blood
> which is my food to eternal life
> but if thou sayest Christ cannot be real flesh
> except he be carnal I say
> thou knowest not the power of God.

We are interested in your use of the word 'real'.
In what way would you distinguish this 'real' Christ
from that which was in Jerusalem?
Do you identify the one with the other?
If not, how would you express the difference?

> Mind, my dear ones in the Lamb,
> that words get not up
> and presumption get afoot
> and so get out from the Simplicity.
> Mind the Babe in thee.

Do you deny the use of Reason? Thomas Bromley
claims to know things by a higher light than reason
even by an extraordinary radiation of the mind.
Would you say that was your experience?
Would not this admit irrationality? Madness?
Would not this lead to danger?

>   If thou meanest carnal knowledge
>   I say it knows not the things of God.

SIXTEEN. London, 1655

The people to whom oppression hath been a burden
have long waited deliverance
but as power is come into the hands of men
it hath been turned to violence.

God is against you
who get great estates
laying house on house
and land on land
until there is no room for the poor.

Now the Lord comes
to require his corn and wine
which he gave to feed the hungry.

Now the Lord comes
to enquire after his wool and flax
which he gave to clothe the naked.

Now is the world turned upside down
and Christ himself is come
to lead his Lambs into the truth.

>   What exactly do you mean by truth?

He that sanctifieth
and they that are sanctified
are one.

Oh James,
do you not hear what you are saying?
Do you not see the danger into which you run?
The tide is turning, James,
mind your guide,
watch the sinking sands,
mind not to go beyond your measure.

There is something drawing towards us, Friends.
See to it.
Beware of striving in thine own will.

SEVENTEEN

Women are making disturbances.
Women are becoming hysterical.
They speak constantly in our Meetings
of childish things. Childishly.

> We are thy lambs, James,
> we feel the power of the Lord in thee
> and it is beautiful. Thy voice
> touches our hearts, our hearts
> yearn towards thee.
> Feed thy lambs, James.

Feed not on knowledge Martha, Dorcas,
Judy, Rebecca, Hannah, Jane.
For whoever feeds on knowledge
dies to the innocent life.

> But we are hungry,
> we are moved of the Spirit,
> look how we quake and tremble!
> The Spirit moves us to speak
> to sing to tremble, how
> should we be silent?

Martha Simmonds fell to singing
in an unclean spirit.
The substance of what she sang was
INNOCENCY INNOCENCY
many times over
for the space of an hour or more.

    INNOCENCY a pure flower
    a white sheet folded over and over
    clear-starched, fresh from the press
    laid on the marriage bed.
    INNOCENCY
    as it was in the beginning
    with a fresh smell like creation
    like the smell of fresh blood
    INNOCENT as the leaves after rain
    as the fine soft hair of the new-born
    INNOCENCY in the nature of all creatures
    all things working together. Oh James
    is there not a unity in creation
    and all things whole and wholly new?
    HOLY HOLY HOLY in the high places
    deep within full of the sound of silence
    full of the taste of yourself
    and the sound of the blood flowing
    the beating of the heart
    the emptiness of the shell
    full of the sound of the sea
    and light sounding like a trumpet in darkness.

    Oh let it all go, let all fall
    let all fall through your fingers
    like a blessing like warm sand
    like soft rain like the long soft rain
    after a long drought
    soaking the roots.

Martha Simmonds
thou speaks in thine own will.
Thou seeks dominion. Thou is run forth
to utter words without knowledge.
Go home and mind thy calling.

>
> Richard Hubberthorne says I must be silent
> Must I be silent, James? Must I not speak?
> Is there not that of God in me?
> Do you not hear the voice of God
> singing in Paradise garden:
> Time to come home dear child,
> nightfall. Time for bed.
>
> Mother, god-mother, Mother of God,
> do you not hear her voice?
> Lead me, James. Give me a leading.
> I look for judgement.

But James is silent. James is weeping.

> I looked for Judgement and behold a cry.
> Behold a cry and behold an oppression.

EIGHTEEN. London, 1655

The Light of Christ I witness revealed in me
GEORGE FOX.

The Light is One
and leads to all Truth
so we are of one mind
in the Truth.

But the truth is
we are not of one mind.

In whom then is the Light of Christ revealed?

In me. GEORGE FOX.

James must bear his own burdens
and his company's with him
whose iniquity doth increase.
They are joined against the Truth
to fulfill their own desires.
Search and consider if this be innocency.

The Light of God in all I own
BUT THIS I JUDGE.

I discern a cloud of darkness risen up in James.
He is much out.

OUT of the truth
out of the way
out of the power
out of the wisdom
and out of the life of God.

This is the word of the Lord to thee, James Nayler.

NINETEEN

IT stands with its legs straddled
horns lowered, belly sunken, tongue lolling.
Light glints on the channels
where the tide is flooding. Hooves sink
until the hamstrings drown
and the wet sand shivers, glistens,
sucks round the hairy shanks.

Over the flat sands of the bay
Furness fells stretch dark on the skyline,
dove-coloured distances, silver, greenish,
ochre and slate fold round that singular
black vertical
on the shining levels.

TWENTY. London, 1655

MARTHA SIMMONDS: seeing James so changed
they concluded I had bewitched him
and set upon me to pluck him away.

It was the desire of Friends
that James should leave the women's company
but he was subject to them.

There did appear a very great alteration in James.

Friends agreed to go with him to Launceston
where George Fox was in prison.

On the passage thither
they were imprisoned in Exeter
but Martha Simmonds went to George
exalted herself and judged him,
said he was Lord and King
that his heart was rotten, she
came singing in his face
inventing words.

He judged her an unclean spirit.

TWENTY-ONE. Launceston, 1655

Old Fox. Dog Fox. Old clever-Dick
hobbety-goblin Fox, old George
he knows which way to jump! He knows
the goings-out, the comings-in,
he knows the short-cuts, back-ways
back-doubles and side-turnings oh
he's sharp is George!
Going to earth his scent is cold
under the hedgerow. Slyboots Fox
he'll wash their blood from off his feet
he'll wade through water and through fire
the hounds will lose the scent.

Atop of Pendle there are witches – what
were you at up Pendle, Fox?
Those who have dealings with the Devil say
his seed is like ice-water.
Who knows thy seed, George?
Does Margaret know thee, Fox,
are you her King?
The Beast, the King of the Beasts
his glass eye squinnies and
he shows his teeth, he's running now
through water and through fire
carrying the fire in his tail
hounds after him singing a peal of bells
over the frost-white fellside's limestone bones
and so to earth.

And does thee hope
to rise again? Born-again Fox
flexible fleetfooted surefooted
infallible various voracious
vixinated obnoxious furious
furtive furry bestial beset
befuddledbefallenfallacious
fuddlingfiddlingabblingobbledegook.

**MARTHA SIMMONDS THE RIGHTEOUS SEED
IS BURDENED WITH THEE.**

TWENTY-TWO. Exeter, July 1656

George sent for James, having something to speak to him
privately, but he would not come.

George asked why he would not come
Something got up in James
and he uttered forth these words:
BEWARE OF LYING AND FALSE WITNESS.

Asked wherein he could charge George
with lying, he said
he did not charge him so, but George
had received lies from others. Asked
why he would not come to George he said
There was love in my heart to him
that would have carried me through fire and water
but there would have been
nothing but strife and contention.

Then he offered George an apple.

> Do you tempt me, James?
> Am I a serpent? There is no knowledge
>   of good or evil
>   but you have it already.
> Can you say you are moved of the Lord?
>   I offer you an apple. Because we are friends,
>   are we not? This is in Truth
>   an apple.
> What are you offering me, James?
>   What kind of Type, Figure or Shadow?
>   What kind of Sign?
> A Ribstone Pippin. In Truth. Take it
>   for Christ's sake.

But George denied it.

Then James, sitting in a place
lower than the rest of the chamber
asked if he might kiss George, and he,
standing above that low place,

would have drawn James up to him
but he would not come.
And George would not bow down to his asking
so gave him his hand to kiss.

> Do you tempt me, George?
> I offer you the hand of brotherhood
>   because we are brothers. Are we not?
> Cain and Abel. Jacob and Esau. What
>   are you offering me?
> My hand.
> What kind of Type, Figure or Shadow?
>   What kind of Sign?
> It is my hand. Take it. For Christ's sake.

But he would not.

So George, still standing above the low place
where James was sitting said
IT IS MY FOOT.

> Thou canst not come to me, James,
> who hath a wrong measure and judgement.
> My own is my own. Thy disciples
> call tricks the power of God.
> Pride and the Boaster is up.
> Thou hast satisfied the world
> and their desires. Search and consider
> if this be innocency.

(INNOCENCY the pure white blossom
the fresh smell like creation
like the smell of fresh blood
a white sheet clear-starched laid on the marriage bed
stained with fresh blood
the time is come
when nothing will satisfy but BLOOD
YEA YEA THE TIME IS COME
when nothing will satisfy but BLOOD.)

TWENTY-THREE. Bristol, October 1656

On the sixth day of the tenth month
between the second and third hour in the afternoon
James and his company came riding through Bedminster
a mile from the city of Bristol.

A young man (one Timothy Wedlocke
of the county of Devon) with his hat off
leading James' horse and one Samuel Carter
(of Ely) with his hat on
and two men (John Stranger and Robert Crab)
riding each with a woman behind him
(Hannah Stranger, wife to John,
and Martha, wife to Thomas Simmonds,
Stationer, of London) and one woman
(Dorcas Erbery) walking the dirty causeway.

One George Witherley
bid them come up on the dry, saying
the Lord required no such extremity at their hands
but they made no answer but sung and kept their way
knee-deep in the mire
it being very rainy and foul weather
they received the rain in at their necks
and vented it at their hose and britches.

When they came to the Liberties
one of the women alighted
and she and the other woman
went one on each side of the horse
in spite of the rain. The women
spread their handkerchiefs and scarves before him
singing Hosannah, Holy holy holy.

And so they led him.
And so he came into town.

They came to the High Cross of Bristol
and up to the White Hart in Broad Street
where the women dried their hair before the fire.

The magistrates being informed
commanded them to be searched
and found divers letters filled
with profane nonsensical language which
were the grounds of their examination.

TWENTY-FOUR. London, November 1656

Upon report of the Magistrates of Bristol, Parliament chose a Committee to take notice of the matter. JN was sent to London with Stranger, his wife Hannah, Martha Simmonds and Dorcas Erbery.

Accused that he did assume the postures, words, honours and worships of Our Blessed Saviour.

Questioned, Dorcas Erbery confessed
that she did spread her garments before him.
Martha Simmonds said she spread her garments before him
in obedience to the Lord.
Hannah Stranger said she threw two handkerchiefs before him
because the Lord commanded her to do so.

Questioned, did they sing Holy Holy Holy before him,
Dorcas Erbery said she did not sing
but they that did were moved of the Lord.
Martha Simmonds being asked did she sing Holy Holy
answered IT IS MY LIFE TO PRAISE THE LORD.
Hannah Stranger said she did not stand there to accuse herself.
Asked what were the songs sung before him,
was the song Holy Holy, JN answered
It may be so. Very likely it was.

Accused that he had assumed the name
and incommunicable attributes of Our Blessed Saviour, viz;
THE FAIREST OF TEN THOUSAND.
Answered, if it was spoken of that
which the Father hath begotten in me
I dare not deny it
for it is beautiful in whomsoever it is begotten.

THE ONLY BEGOTTEN SON OF GOD.
Accused that Hannah Stranger gave him that title
answered that he was indeed the Son of God
and had many brethren.

THE PROPHET OF THE MOST HIGH.
Asked, was he the prophet of the Most High
answered that he was a prophet
but there were many prophets beside him.

KING OF ISRAEL:
Asked, did he own the name King of Israel
answered, I have no kingdom in this world
but a Kingdom I have.
And he that hath redeemed me
hath redeemed me for ever.

JESUS: evidence that John Stranger used these words:
Thy name is no more to be called James but Jesus.
Answered, I understood he gave the name of Jesus
to the Christ that is in me.

THE LAMB OF GOD: answered, If I were not the Lamb of God
I should not be so sought after to be devoured.

CONCLUDED: that JN did assume the postures, words, honours
worships and miracles of Our Blessed Saviour.

Asked, did he reprove the women for spreading their garments
and singing, answered, If they had it from the Lord
who am I that I should judge?

> I do abhor that any of the honour due to God
> should be given to me
> but it hath pleased the Lord to set me up
> as a sign of the coming of the Righteous One
> and what was done as I passed through Bristol
> I was commanded of the Lord to suffer.
>
> There was never anything since I was born
> so much against my will and judgement
> as this thing
>
> for I knew I should lay down my life for it.

Upon Wednesday November 25th the Committee met and agreed to
deliver their report which they did upon the 4th December.

TWENTY-FIVE. London, December 1656

EXTRACT FROM THE INSTRUMENT OF GOVERNMENT 1653: that such as profess faith in God by Jesus Christ, though differing in judgement from the doctrine publicly held forth, should be protected in profession of faith and exercise of their religion, so they abuse not this liberty to the injury of others or the disturbance of the public peace.

> I would spend my blood upon the Instrument of Government
> but if it hold anything to protect such persons
> I would have it burnt in the fire.
>
> If you make the sentence death
> he very well deserves it.
>
> Should we not be as jealous of God's honour
> as of our own? Shall we suffer the Lord Jesus Christ
> to be abused? This is horrid blasphemy.
>
> It is deposing the image of God.
> It is the un-godding of God.
>
> We cannot show too great a detestation of it.
>
> It is said we have no law against blasphemy
> but where there is a law what is the punishment?
> Is it less than death?
>
> If be the law of God that this person should die
> we ought not to spare him. For my part
> I think there is no such law.
>
> We are under Gospel administration
> and no warrant can be found for his punishment.
> The inward thoughts of men
> are not to be punished in this world.
>
> If we judge by Christian rules
> the other persons are more guilty than he,
> they gave him the honour.

He did admonish the people not to do anything
but what God commanded them.
I would have this used in extenuation.

This business lies heavy on my heart.
If you hang every man who says Christ is in him
you will hang a good many.

If Nayler be a blasphemer
so are all the generation of Quakers
and must undergo the same punishment.

What sticks with me is the nearness of this thing
to the Glorious Truth, that the Spirit is in us.

The Instrument of Government says
all must be protected that profess faith in Jesus Christ
which I suppose this man doth.

As to the Instrument of Government I hope
it will not be used as an argument
to let the wretch escape.

I cannot give my vote to pass sentence of death.
I doubt you, having no law, can properly do it.

I would have it regular.

We ought to be zealous of God
but our Zeal should go by the rule.

It is Horrid Blasphemy.

Let us all stop our ears and hang him.

FOR THE SENTENCE OF DEATH:

Yes: 82   No: 96.

TWENTY-SIX. London, December 1656

RESOLVED: That James Nayler be set with his head in the pillory in the new Palace Yard, Westminster during the space of two hours next Thursday and be whipped by the hangman through the streets of Westminster to Old Exchange, London, and there likewise be set with his head in the pillory for the space of two hours between the hours of eleven and one on Saturday next wearing a paper containing the inscription of his crimes and that at the Old Exchange his tongue shall be bored through with a red-hot iron and that he be there also stigmatised on the forehead with the letter B and that he be afterwards sent to Bristol and conveyed into and through the said city on a horse bare-ridged with his face backwards and there also publicly whipped the next market day after he comes thither and from thence he be committed to Bridewell, London and there be restrained from the society of all people and there to labour hard until he be released by Parliament and during the time be debarred from the use of pen, ink and paper and shall have no relief but what he earns by his daily labour.

> God hath given me a body.
> He will I hope give me the spirit to endure it.
> The Lord lay not these things to your charge.
> I shall pray he will not.

December 20th, 1656

> They whipped him from Westminster to Old Exchange.
> There was not so much as the breadth of a man's nail
> between his stripes. Three hundred and ten lashes.
> He was much abused with the horses treading on him
> the prints of the nails being seen upon his feet.

> A delay was petitioned in carrying out the rest of the sentence:
> That James Nayler being in a very ill and dangerous condition
> not fit to undergo the sentence he is adjudged
> we beg a respite that he may recover a little strength.

> A week's delay was granted.

December 27th, 1656

> This day James Nayler received the second part of his sentence.
> He behaved himself very handsomely and patiently,

put out his tongue willingly
but shrinked a little when the hot iron came on his forehead.
It was very remarkable that notwithstanding
there was a great crowd of people they were very quiet
few heard to revile him
or seen to throw anything at him.
When he was burned
all the people before him and behind him
and on both sides
with one consent
stood bareheaded.

TWENTY-SEVEN. Bristol, December 1656

    Cause him to ride in at Lawfordsgate
    along Wine Street to the Tolsey
    then down High Street over the bridge
    and so out at Redcliffe Gate.
    So bring him into Thomas Street
    there cause him to be stripped
    and made fast to a cart-horse
    and in the market first whipped.

    Thence to the foot of the bridge
    there whipped
    thence to the end of the bridge
    there whipped
    thence to the middle of High Street
    there whipped
    thence to the Tolsey
    there whipped
    thence to the middle of Broad Street
    there whipped.

    Thence to the Taylor's Hall
    there release him from the cart-horse
    and put on his clothes.

TWENTY-EIGHT. Bridewell, London, 1657

JN is in Bridewell. He is still
in separation from the Truth
but the Truth will work through all.

The women are exceedingly filthy
acting imitations and singing. They appoint
Meetings in the places where James suffered.
At the Bull and Mouth they broke bread
and took wine
saying it was to manifest
they had love to the wicked.

The Power of Darkness is over them.

> You said there would be suffering, James
> before there could be rejoicing.
> Now there is suffering. Weakness pain fear
> helplessness heartbreak. Men
> took away our voices
> but we are crying out now
> crying aloud now
> crying for the Kingdom
> the Kingdom of Heaven
> Now.
>
> There has been suffering. Now
> there will be rejoicing James
> there will be rejoicing.
> Now.

Oh Martha. Martha. My heart
is broken this day.

JN is in a suffering condition
of spirit as of body. A great darkness
is over him. They will let few come to him
but his wife gets to him sometimes.

TWENTY-NINE. Wakefield, 1657

ANNE NAYLER:

Good hay off top field. Rain held up
and it dried well. Loft full.
A dozen hens to Wakefield with the cheese
not worth the trouble. Made candles.
Four shillings owed the blacksmith. Lambs
went off with Jackson, he will get a price.
Daisy to Sam's old bull. Roofing the byre.
Tom shaping well. Made soap and ale.
Good malting barley this year. Hannah poorly.

Snow over Christmas but it didn't lie.
London for James. His tongue's nigh healed
but his brow's badly yet. He was very low.
I saw that Martha. I could have told him
he'd not have heeded. Parted kindly.

THIRTY. Bridewell, 1657

My heart is broken this day
for the offence I have committed to God's truth.

Not minding in all things to stay single and low
I was drawn out of the constant watch
and darkness came upon me.

Having lost my own guide
I gave myself up wholly to be led by others.

I was beset with darkness
chased out as a wandering Bird gone from her nest
into the world as a sign
and as far as I gave advantage
through want of judgement
for that evil spirit to rise
I take shame on myself justly.

I entreat you
to speak to those I have most offended
and in the spirit of Jesus Christ
I am willing to confess the offence.

Will you forgive me, George?

If I know anything of the Spirit
it naturally inclines to mercy and forgiveness
and not to bind one another to the nearest farthing
(though this be just and I do not condemn it)
but delights in forgiving debts.

Forgive and forget?
George?

    James, you are already forgotten.

THIRTY-ONE. London, 1658

WHAT THE PROFESSION OF THE LIVING FAITH IS.

I see that which loves the things of this world
to be none of his love.
Nor that his joy that takes pleasure in carnal things
nor that his liberty that is in the works of the flesh
nor that his peace that is in sin
nor that his patience that takes its own revenge
nor that his glory that's in pride
nor that his wisdom that's after the flesh
nor that his fear that's taught by the precepts of men
These are of the world
they are not in him.

Wait low and diligently
until that thing spring up
which is felt far below all fleshly affections
so you cannot come to the life and spring of it
but as you deny them

and let the little thing
that is pure and simple
lead you

and be not discouraged because of the littleness
for you know not the power it hath with God

for though you come through great temptations
yet shall not one grain of the seed perish

but into the likeness of his death you must come
that the fellowship of his suffering you may feel.

THIRTY-TWO

They said I was Jesus Christ
the Fairest of Ten Thousand
the Only Begotten Son of God
the Prophet of the Most High
He in whom the hope of Israel standeth
the Lamb of God
the Son of God
Jesus.

And as I took all this upon me
so I took their sin upon me
and his suffering upon me
and only the Everlasting Son of Righteousness
the Lamb of God
the Son of God
Jesus
could carry that cross.

    Are you still suffering under that delusion?

I am witness to that truth:
the Son of God suffered in me
and died in me
and in me now rises to eternal life.

    That's blasphemy, James.

THIRTY-THREE

EDWARD DEWSBURY: In the fullness of time I was led of the Lord
into London. In that day the Lord healed up the
breach which had long been a sadness in the
hearts of many.

        The Lord clothed the hearts of my dear brothers
        with precious wisdom. And dear James
        the Lord was with him.

RICHARD HUBBERTHORNE to GEORGE FOX:
        I gave James thy letter
        he doth remember his dear love to thee
        and doth desire to hear from thee
        whether anything be upon thee concerning him.

        This is the word of the Lord to thee
        James Nayler:
        Go North.
        Go home.

        Go North out of the way.

THIRTY-FOUR. Huntingdon, October 1660

So James goes North because
George says he must and James
is not minded any longer
to stand in his own will.

Past Tyburn into Finchley, Barnet, Hatfield,
and on to Lechworth, Biggleswade, Sandy, St Neots,
a long road. Featureless. Fields lie fallow
under autumn rains. Blackberries shrivel
along the hedgerows. Spires of churches rise
from the long levels to the flat white sky.

Outside Huntingdon where the Great Ouse
wanders through watermeadows he is seen
(by a Friend of Hertford) sitting by the road
in such an awful frame of mind
as if he had been redeemed from the earth
and was a stranger to it.

Trousers tied with string
coat ripped at the seams, hat over brow
and rain soaking the sacking on his shoulders.
A travelling man. He gazes at his boots.
Three or four sparky lads (Jesus he stinks!
Dare you go up to him? Go on, I dare you!)
Do they call you Jesus? That your name? Jesus?
One punches him, another jostles,
he's in the ditch. You got no home to go to?
Get moving, Jesus man. Get going. OUT!

They'd meant no harm, they said.
We just said what's your name? And he said
Nothing. Nothing. And a willingness there is
to be nothing. He wept then and the tears
ran down the mud on his face.

Someone came past, come evening,
took him to village. Dr Parnell came round
(being a Friend) but he was too far gone.

And not long after
departed this life
in the peace of God
and was buried in the garden.

THIRTY-FIVE. Wakefield, 1660

ANNE NAYLER.
Pigs killed out well. Made puddings. Brawn.
Cured hams. Sarah right handy. Mary bad,
a spotted fever and she's not right yet.
Spinning. Fox got two hens. Raining,
fixed roof again, the timber rotten.
Brought stock in-bye. First frosts held off
'til now. Got word from Friends James died
Huntingdon way. A long hard road is that
black soil, birch, hazel coppice. Poor James.
Better he'd stayed at home and died in bed.
I would have mourned him then.

THIRTY-SIX. Popular Remembrance

And now the time of the examination is come
and, the questions being set before you
(as in the old familiar nightmare),
you can answer none of them.

Could you not even write your name?

The name given to him by the world was James Nayler.

You may remember that he was an obscure Quaker
who rode naked through the streets of Bristol
causing a public scandal. Certain hysterical women
hailed him with cries of Holy Holy Holy
and waved palm before him, deluding him
into thinking he was Jesus Christ.

He was hung drawn and quartered
burned at the stake
and wrote a dying oration.

You may remember these things
they are not altogether true
and may seem hardly worth recalling.

Why do you write nothing?
Can you not make yourself clear?

The clarity comes after the fear
and leads to the courage.
It is beyond words.

If you don't feel you can go so far
as to write your name
you can sign with a cross.